"Everybody can be great, because everybody can serve. You don't have to have a college degree to serve. You don't have to make your subject and your verb agree to serve. You don't have to know about Plato and Aristotle to serve. You don't have to know Einstein's theory of relativity to serve. You don't have to know the second theory of thermodynamics in physics to serve. You only need a heart full of grace, a soul generated by love."
—Martin Luther King Jr.

BE A KING

DR. MARTIN LUTHER KING JR.'S DREAM AND YOU

CAROLE BOSTON WEATHERFORD

ILLUSTRATED BY
JAMES E. RANSOME

BLOOMSBURY
CHILDREN'S BOOKS
NEW YORK LONDON OXFORD NEW DELHI SYDNEY

BLOOMSBURY CHILDREN'S BOOKS
Bloomsbury Publishing Inc., part of Bloomsbury Publishing Plc
1385 Broadway, New York, NY 10018

BLOOMSBURY, BLOOMSBURY CHILDREN'S BOOKS, and the Diana logo are trademarks of Bloomsbury Publishing Plc

First published in the United States of America in January 2018 by Bloomsbury Children's Books
Paperback edition published in January 2022

Text copyright © 2018 by Carole Boston Weatherford
Illustrations copyright © 2018 by James E. Ransome

Bloomsbury books may be purchased for business or promotional use. For information on bulk purchases please contact Macmillan Corporate and Premium Sales Department at specialmarkets@macmillan.com

ISBN 978-1-5476-0897-3 (paperback)

The Library of Congress has cataloged the hardcover edition as follows:
Names: Weatherford, Carole Boston, author. | Ransome, James, illustrator.
Title: Be a king : Dr. Martin Luther King Jr.'s dream and you / Carole Boston Weatherford ; illustrated by James Ransome.
Description: New York : Bloomsbury USA Children's, 2018.
Identifiers: LCCN 2017019952 (print) | LCCN 2017032825 (e-book)
ISBN 978-0-8027-2368-0 (hardcover) • ISBN 978-1-68119-195-9 (e-book) • ISBN 978-1-68119-196-6 (e-PDF)
Subjects: LCSH: King, Martin Luther, Jr., 1929–1968—Juvenile literature. | African Americans—Biography—Juvenile literature. | Civil rights workers—United States—Biography—Juvenile literature. | African Americans—Civil rights—History—20th century—Juvenile literature. | Civil rights movements—United States—History—20th century—Juvenile literature. | BISAC: JUVENILE NONFICTION / Biography & Autobiography / Historical. | JUVENILE NONFICTION / History / United States / 20th Century. | JUVENILE NONFICTION / People & Places / United States / African American.
Classification: LCC E185.97.K5 (e-book) | LCC E185.97.K5 W44 2018 (print) |
DDC 323.092 [B]—dc23
LC record available at https://lccn.loc.gov/2017019952

Painted with acrylics, colored pencils, oils, and gouache • Typeset in Baskerville and Rockwell • Book design by Heather Palisi
Printed in China by Leo Paper Products, Heshan, Guangdong
2 4 6 8 10 9 7 5 3 1

To find out more about our authors and books visit www.bloomsbury.com and sign up for our newsletters.

"Service is the rent we pay for the privilege of living on this earth."
—Congresswoman Shirley Chisholm

To everyone who marched, protested, and stood up for
civil rights for all Americans. —J. E. R.

You can be a King.

Marvel at creation.

Keep the faith of your ancestors.

You can be a King.

Know that bigotry hurts.
Remember how you felt
when treated unfairly.

You can be a King.

Admit that you've done wrong.

Just say, "I'm sorry," and mean it.

You can be a King.

Know that dividing walls should come down.

You have glimpsed the other side.

You can be a King.

Break the chains of ignorance.

Learn as much as you can.

You can be a King.

Stand for peace.

Band together against bullies.

You can be a King.

Sing a song of freedom.

Keep your eyes on the prize; hold on.

You can be a King.

Stamp out hatred.

Put your foot down and walk tall.

You can be a King.

Answer your critics.

Believe in your cause and state it plainly.

You can be a King.

Have a dream.

Make yours great enough to grow into.

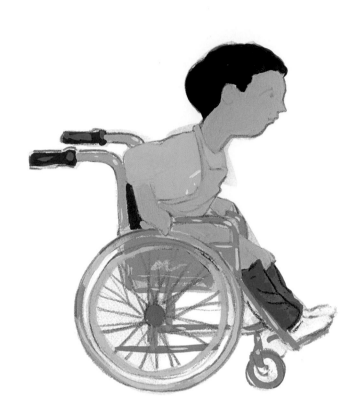

You can be a King.

Make the world take notice.

Do your very best at whatever you do.

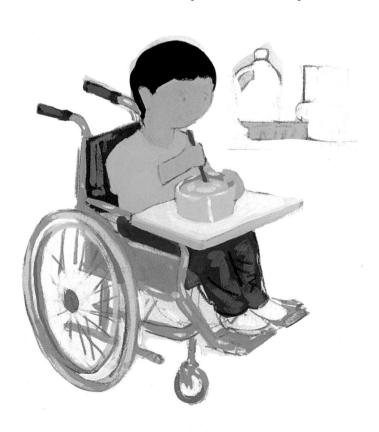

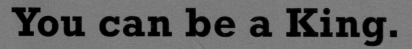
You can be a King.
Lift up the less fortunate.
Be the King or Queen of Help.

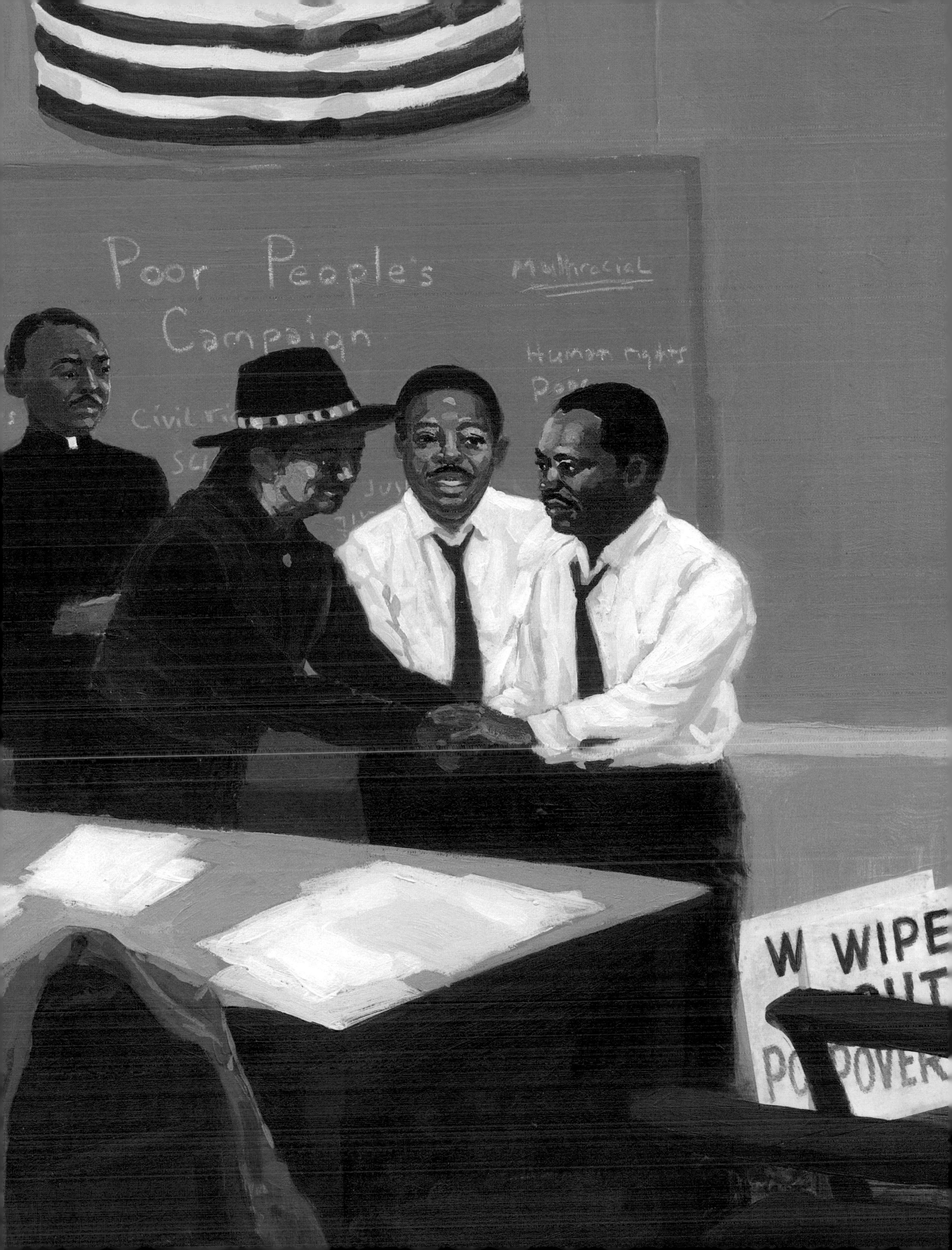
Poor People's Campaign
Multiracial
Human rights
WIPE

You can be a King.

Set your sights on the mountaintop.

Climb a little higher every day.

Author's Note

There was nothing in Martin Luther King Jr.'s beginnings to hint that he would become a great humanitarian. Born into a family of Baptist preachers in 1929, Martin Luther King Jr. grew up in Atlanta's segregated Sweet Auburn neighborhood. He first felt the sting of racism at age six when a white friend told him they could no longer play together. At age twelve, he jumped out of a window after his grandmother died while he was attending a parade without permission. In 1944, during a summer in Connecticut, he witnessed racial integration for the first time.

That fall, at age fifteen, he entered Morehouse College under a wartime early-admissions policy. There, he was influenced by college president Benjamin Mays, who called on Black churches to take up social causes. In 1948, King went on to Crozer Theological Seminary in Pennsylvania, where he learned of Mohandas Gandhi's nonviolent philosophy of civil disobedience. At Crozer, King was elected the first Black student-body president. He went on to earn a doctorate degree from Boston University. While in Boston, he met Coretta Scott, his future wife, who was studying to be a concert singer.

Soon after becoming pastor of Dexter Avenue Baptist Church in Montgomery, Alabama, King stepped into history. He was enlisted to lead the bus boycott that began when seamstress and NAACP secretary Rosa Parks was arrested for refusing to give up her seat to a white man on a city bus. After the successful 381-day boycott, King cofounded the Southern Christian Leadership Conference to organize civil rights protests throughout the South. In 1960, he returned to Atlanta to copastor at Ebenezer Baptist Church with his father and devote himself full time to the civil rights movement. That same year, he was arrested at a student-led lunch counter sit-in.

In 1963, community leaders summoned King to fight segregation in Birmingham, Alabama—a city nicknamed "Bombingham" for a string of unsolved racially motivated bombings. During those protests, police turned high-pressure hoses and canine dogs on marchers. While jailed for his role in those marches, King wrote his eloquent "Letter from Birmingham Jail," in response

to white clergy's pleas for him to halt the marches and wait patiently for change. Later that year, he delivered his rousing "I Have a Dream" speech before a crowd of 250,000 at the historic March on Washington for Jobs and Freedom. In 1964, the year that Congress passed the Civil Rights Act, King was awarded the Nobel Peace Prize.

In 1965, he led the Selma to Montgomery March—actually a series of three marches—which marked the political and emotional peak of the modern civil rights movement. The first march, on March 7, ended after only six blocks when police beat back the nonviolent protesters at Edmund Pettus Bridge with tear gas and billy clubs. That day became known as Bloody Sunday. Two days later, King led a symbolic march to the bridge, where protesters kneeled in prayer. The third march lasted five days and reached Montgomery with 25,000 protesters on March 25. Those marches led to passage of the Voting Rights Act of 1965.

For leading mass protests, King was jailed numerous times and targeted by white racists with knives and bombs. At the same time, some Black preachers considered him a troublemaker and more militant Black leaders rejected his nonviolent approach.

King kept marching, though, and pursuing his humanitarian mission. He spoke out against the United States role in the war in Vietnam. And he fought discrimination in housing, employment, and schools. That fight took him to Memphis, Tennessee, in April 1968 to support striking sanitation workers. While there, he gave his prophetic "Mountaintop" speech, in which he alluded to the Promised Land and the possibility of his own premature death. On the evening of April 4, 1968, he was assassinated. Riots broke out in more than 120 American cities. His funeral was an international event.

In 1983, a national holiday—to be observed on the third Monday in January—was proclaimed in his honor.

CAROLE BOSTON WEATHERFORD has authored many children's books, including *Jesse Owens: Fastest Man Alive*; *I, Matthew Henson: Polar Explorer*; and *Be a King: Dr. Martin Luther King Jr.'s Dream and You*. Her books have been recognized with two NAACP Image Awards, a Newbery Honor, three Caldecott Honors, a Charlotte Zolotow Award, a Coretta Scott King Author Honor, a WNDB Walter Award, and numerous other awards. She is a professor at Fayetteville State University in North Carolina.

CBWeatherford.com

JAMES E. RANSOME has illustrated many picture books, including *Be a King: Dr. Martin Luther King Jr.'s Dream and You*. He received his BFA from Pratt Institute in New York, and his books have garnered numerous accolades including the Coretta Scott King Award for Illustration for *The Creation*, three Coretta Scott King Illustrator Honors, a Boston Globe–Horn Book Honor, an ALA Notable Book Selection, a Jane Addams Children's Book Award, and an NAACP Image Award. James lives in Rhinebeck, New York, with his wife, author Lesa Cline-Ransome.

jamesransome.com